By the Editors of Best Recipes

Best Recipes

CHICKEN

COOKBOOK

SMITHMARK

Louis Weber, C.E.O.
Publications International, Ltd.
7373 North Cicero Avenue
Lincolnwood, Illinois 60646

Permission is never granted for commercial purposes.

This edition published in 1991 by SMITHMARK Publishers Inc.,
112 Madison Avenue, New York, NY 10016

Photography on pages 13, 39, 43 and 93 by Vuksanovich/Chicago.

Remaining photography by Sacco Productions Limited/Chicago.
Photographers: Catherine Money
              Laurie Proffitt
Photo Stylist/Production: Paula Walters
Food Stylists: Janice Bell
           Donna Coates

ISBN: 0-8317-0596-5

Library of Congress Catalog Card Number: 90-63052

Pictured on the front cover: Apricot Chicken Oriental (*page 58*).

Pictured on the back cover (*clockwise from top left*): Bittersweet Farm Chicken (*page 56*), Chicken and Walnut Salad Athena (*page 18*), Calorie-Wise Dill Chicken (*page 66*), and Stir-Fried Chicken (*page 48*).

First published in the United States.

Manufactured in Yugoslavia.

8 7 6 5 4 3 2 1

SMITHMARK books are available for bulk purchase for sales promotion and premium use.
For details write or telelphone the Manager of Special Sales, SMITHMARK Publishers Inc.,
112 Madison Avenue, New York, NY 10016. (212) 532-6600

By the Editors of Best Recipes

Best Recipes

CHICKEN

COOKBOOK

CHICKEN BASICS

Chicken is a mainstay in the American diet. And now, more than ever before, it is appearing at meals with increasing frequency. Low in fat, calories and price, chicken has a universal taste appeal that can't be beat. It is also extremely versatile, lending itself to almost every type of cooking.

If you find yourself preparing chicken dishes more than once a week, you will appreciate this unique collection of award-winning chicken recipes. Gathered from a variety of cooking contests across America, it represents some of the very best offerings in chicken cookery—original dishes created by home cooks like you. The names of these champion home cooks, as well as the contests they entered, are included for all the delectable recipes.

Every recipe in this book uses broiling/frying chickens. These are young birds that range in size from 1½ to 4 pounds. Tender and mildly flavored, they are best when broiled, fried, roasted or sautéed.

Storing Chicken

Fresh, uncooked chicken can be refrigerated for up to two days. If the chicken you purchase comes packaged in plastic bags or on plastic-sealed trays, it may be refrigerated in the original packaging. If the chicken comes wrapped in butcher paper, unwrap and repackage it airtight in plastic bags or plastic wrap. When you are ready to cook the chicken, rinse it under cold water, pat dry with paper towels and trim away any excess fat.

If the chicken you purchase will not be cooked within two days, it should be frozen. To properly freeze chicken, remove it from its original packaging. Rinse it under cold water, pat dry with paper towels and trim away any excess fat. For a whole chicken, remove the giblets from the body cavity. Wrap the chicken in moisture-proof freezer paper, label it with the date and freeze. Wrap, label and freeze the giblets separately. Use this same procedure to freeze chicken pieces, but separate the pieces into several packages so they freeze quickly. Freeze whole chickens for up to eight months, chicken pieces for up to six months and giblets for up to three months.

The best way to defrost uncooked frozen chicken is to thaw it in its wrapping in the refrigerator. Allow enough time for it to thaw completely, about three to four hours per pound. *Never* defrost chicken on the countertop at room temperature. The outside of the chicken will thaw before the inside, increasing the possibility of harmful bacterial growth on the thawed portions.

Testing for Doneness

There are several ways to test chicken to see if it is completely cooked. The most accurate method for whole chickens is to use a meat thermometer. Before roasting, insert the thermometer into the thickest part of the inner thigh away from any bones. The chicken is done when the temperature registers 180°F. Temperature can also be measured with a handy, instant reading thermometer that is inserted just before a reading is taken and is then removed. Insert this thermometer into the thigh as described above. To test chicken pieces, insert a fork into the thickest part of the piece. If the fork goes in easily, the juices are clear, not pink, and the chicken is tender throughout, then it is fully cooked.

Chicken Preparation Tips

—Thoroughly wash cutting surfaces, utensils and your hands with hot soapy water after coming in contact with uncooked chicken. This eliminates the risk of contaminating other foods with salmonella bacteria that is often present in raw chicken. Salmonella is killed during cooking.

—Regardless of the cooking method used, always cook chicken completely. *Do not* partially cook it and then store it to finish cooking later.

—When a recipe calls for chopped cooked chicken, it can be difficult to judge how much chicken to purchase. As a guideline, two whole chicken breasts (about 10 ounces each) will yield about 2 cups of chopped cooked chicken; one broiling/frying chicken (about 3 pounds) will yield about 2½ cups chopped cooked chicken.

—When stuffing a chicken, allow about ¾ cup of stuffing for each pound of chicken.

—When sautéing boneless chicken breasts or other chicken pieces, use a shallow skillet if you want the chicken to stay crisp. A deep pan creates steam, causing a build up of moisture and a loss of crispness.

—Always use tongs to turn chicken pieces over when frying, broiling or grilling. This prevents the skin from being pierced keeping the natural juices sealed inside the skin.

—See page 44 for directions on how to bone chicken breasts.

APPETIZERS & SALADS

Peeling Garlic Cloves

To peel whole garlic cloves, trim off the ends and drop cloves into boiling water for 5 to 10 seconds. Immediately plunge into cold water, then drain. The peels should slip right off. If the cloves are to be minced, trim off the ends and crush with the bottom of a heavy saucepan or the flat side of a large knife. The peels can then be easily removed.

Garlicky Gilroy Chicken Wings

♦ Winifred Harano from Los Angeles, California was the first place winner in the Great Garlic Recipe Contest, sponsored by the Fresh Garlic Association in association with the Gilroy Garlic Festival, Gilroy, California.

Makes about 6 appetizer servings

   2 pounds chicken wings (about 15 wings)
   3 heads fresh garlic,* separated into cloves
       and peeled
   1 cup plus 1 tablespoon olive oil, divided
10 to 15 drops Tabasco pepper sauce
   1 cup grated Parmesan cheese
   1 cup Italian-style bread crumbs
   1 teaspoon black pepper

Preheat oven to 375°F. Disjoint chicken wings, removing tips. (If desired, save tips to make chicken stock.) Rinse wings; pat dry. Place garlic, 1 cup oil and the pepper sauce in food processor or blender container; cover and process until smooth. Pour garlic mixture into small bowl. Combine cheese, bread crumbs and black pepper in shallow dish. Dip wings into garlic mixture, then roll, one at a time, in crumb mixture until thoroughly coated. Brush shallow nonstick pan with remaining 1 tablespoon oil; arrange wings in a single layer. Drizzle remaining garlic mixture over wings; sprinkle with remaining crumb mixture. Bake 45 to 60 minutes or until brown and crisp. Garnish as desired.

*The whole garlic bulb is called a head.

Mozzarella is a soft white cheese that melts easily. In southern Italy, where it originated, it is made from the milk of buffaloes. In other parts of Italy and in North America, it is made from cows' milk.

Chicken Pizza

♦ Mary Cerami of California was a prize winner in the National Chicken Cooking Contest, sponsored by the National Broiler Council.

Makes 8 appetizer servings

- 1 package (8 ounces) refrigerated crescent dinner rolls
- 2 whole chicken breasts, split, skinned and boned
- ¼ cup vegetable oil
- 1 large onion, sliced into thin rings
- 1 large green bell pepper, sliced into thin rings
- ½ pound fresh mushrooms, sliced
- ½ cup pitted ripe olives, sliced
- 1 can (10½ ounces) pizza sauce with cheese
- 1 teaspoon garlic salt
- 1 teaspoon dried oregano
- ¼ cup grated Parmesan cheese
- 2 cups (8 ounces) shredded mozzarella cheese

Preheat oven to 425°F. Separate crescent dough into 8 triangles. Press triangles into lightly oiled 12-inch pizza pan, covering it completely. Cut chicken into 1-inch pieces. Heat oil in large skillet over medium-high heat. Add chicken, onion, green pepper, mushrooms and olives. Cook and stir about 5 minutes or until chicken is cooked. Spread pizza sauce over dough. Spoon chicken mixture evenly over sauce. Sprinkle with garlic salt, oregano and Parmesan cheese. Top with mozzarella cheese. Bake 20 minutes or until crust is golden brown.

Dipper's Nuggets Chicken

♦ Norma Young from Arkansas was a prize winner in the National Chicken Cooking Contest, sponsored by the National Broiler Council.

Makes 8 appetizer servings

  2 **whole chicken breasts, split, skinned and boned**
    Vegetable oil
  1 **egg**
⅓ **cup water**
⅓ **cup all-purpose flour**
  2 **teaspoons sesame seeds**
1½ **teaspoons salt**
    Dipping Sauces (recipes follow)
    Red onion rings, for garnish

Cut chicken into 1-inch pieces. Heat 3 inches oil in large heavy saucepan over medium-high heat until oil reaches 375°F; adjust heat to maintain temperature. Meanwhile, beat egg and water in large bowl until well mixed. Add flour, sesame seeds and salt, stirring to form smooth batter. Dip chicken pieces into batter, draining off excess. Fry chicken, a few pieces at a time, in hot oil about 4 minutes or until golden brown. Drain on paper towels. Serve with Dipping Sauces; garnish with onion rings.

Dipping Sauces

Nippy Pineapple Sauce: Mix 1 jar (12 ounces) pineapple preserves, ¼ cup prepared mustard and ¼ cup prepared horseradish in small saucepan. Cook and stir over low heat 5 minutes.

Dill Sauce: Combine ½ cup sour cream, ½ cup mayonnaise, 2 tablespoons finely chopped dill pickle and 1 teaspoon dill weed in small bowl. Cover; refrigerate 1 hour.

Royalty Sauce: Combine 1 cup catsup, 6 tablespoons butter or margarine, 2 tablespoons vinegar, 1 tablespoon brown sugar and ½ teaspoon dry mustard in small saucepan. Cook and stir over low heat 5 minutes.

Fiesta Potato Flan Olé!

♦ Shirley DeSantis from East Windsor, New Jersey was the first place winner in the "No Small Potatoes" Contest, sponsored by *Family Circle* magazine.

Makes 8 to 10 appetizer or 4 to 6 main-course servings

    3 medium-size russet potatoes (about
        1 pound), cooked and mashed
    ½ cup all-purpose flour
    ¼ cup yellow cornmeal
    4 tablespoons olive oil, divided
    ½ teaspoon garlic salt
    ½ teaspoon pepper
    1 jar (8 ounces) mild picante sauce
    1 cup shredded cooked chicken
    1 cup (4 ounces) shredded Monterey Jack
        cheese with jalapeño peppers
    1 tablespoon chopped parsley
        Guacamole or sour cream, for garnish

Preheat oven to 350°F. Combine warm potatoes, flour, cornmeal, 3 tablespoons of the oil, the garlic salt and pepper in large bowl; mix to form smooth dough. Press onto bottom and up side of ungreased 10-inch flan or quiche pan with removable bottom. Spread picante sauce evenly over potato mixture; top with chicken and cheese. Sprinkle parsley and remaining 1 tablespoon oil over the top. Bake 20 to 25 minutes or until thoroughly heated. Remove ring from pan. Cut flan into wedges and serve garnished with guacamole or sour cream.

The marvelous macadamia nut is second to none for its buttery smooth flavor and delectable crunch. It is the world's most expensive nut and considered by many to also be the world's finest. Native to Australia, the macadamia tree was named after the man who cultivated it, chemist John MacAdam. It was brought to Hawaii in the late nineteenth century and has since become the state's third-largest crop.

Tropical Chicken Salad

♦ Mary Caldwell Clark from Nashville, Tennessee was the third prize winner in the Savory category of the International Association of Cooking Professionals Recipe Contest, sponsored by Coco Lopez® Cream of Coconut, a product of Borden, Inc.

Makes 4 servings

   Tropical Salad Dressing (recipe follows)
 3 **cups cubed cooked chicken**
 ¾ **cup coarsely chopped celery**
 ¾ **cup seedless red or green grape halves**
 ¾ **cup coarsely chopped macadamia nuts or toasted almonds**
   Lettuce leaves
   Strawberries and kiwifruit, for garnish
   Toasted coconut flakes, for garnish

Prepare Tropical Salad Dressing. Combine chicken, celery, grapes and nuts in large bowl; stir in 1 cup of the dressing. Cover; refrigerate 1 hour. Mound chicken salad on lettuce-lined platter or individual plates. Garnish with strawberries, kiwifruit and coconut flakes.

Tropical Salad Dressing: Place ½ cup cream of coconut, ⅓ cup red wine vinegar, 1 teaspoon dry mustard, 1 teaspoon salt and 1 clove garlic in food processor or blender container. With processor on, slowly add 1 cup vegetable oil, processing until smooth. (Refrigerate remaining dressing and serve with fruit or mixed green salads.)

Hot Chinese Chicken Salad

♦ Fayne Lutz from New Mexico was a prize winner in the National Chicken Cooking Contest, sponsored by the National Broiler Council.

Makes 4 servings

    8 chicken thighs, skinned, boned and cut into
        bite-sized pieces
    ¼ cup cornstarch
    ¼ cup vegetable oil
    1 large ripe tomato, cut into pieces
    1 can (4 ounces) water chestnuts, drained and
        sliced
    1 can (4 ounces) sliced mushrooms, drained
    1 cup coarsely chopped green onions
    1 cup diagonally sliced celery
    ¼ cup soy sauce
    1 teaspoon monosodium glutamate
    ⅛ teaspoon garlic powder
    2 cups finely shredded iceberg lettuce
      Orange slices, for garnish
      Hot cooked rice

Dredge chicken, one piece at a time, in cornstarch. Heat oil in wok or large skillet over medium-high heat. Add chicken; stir-fry about 3 minutes or until browned. Add tomato, water chestnuts, mushrooms, green onions, celery, soy sauce, monosodium glutamate and garlic powder. Cover; simmer 5 minutes. Place lettuce on large serving plate. Top with chicken mixture; garnish with orange slices. Serve immediately with rice.

*T*he size of an olive is no indication of its flavor. Some tiny varieties are bitter while others are quite mild, and the same is true for the large ones. Green olives are harvested before they are fully ripe; black olives have ripened on the tree. Both kinds must be cured in brine in order to be fit to eat.

Chicken and Walnut Salad Athena

♦ Eleanor Froehlich from Rochester Hills, Michigan was a finalist in the Hidden Valley Ranch®/California Ripe Olive ''Tastes of the West'' Cooking Contest, sponsored by the California Olive Industry, Fresno, California.

Makes 6 servings

Hidden Valley Ranch® Lemon Herb Dressing (recipe follows)
2 cups cubed cooked chicken breast
2 tablespoons thinly sliced green onions
1 tablespoon minced parsley
2 tablespoons butter or margarine
½ teaspoon dried rosemary, finely crushed
1 cup walnut halves
6 radishes, sliced
12 California ripe olives, sliced
1 cup (4 ounces) fresh feta cheese, crumbled
3 small ripe tomatoes, cut into wedges
Crisp salad greens

Prepare Hidden Valley Ranch® Lemon Herb Dressing. Place chicken in large bowl; pour dressing over chicken. Add green onions and parsley; mix gently. Cover; marinate in refrigerator at least 1 hour or overnight.

Melt butter with rosemary in small heavy skillet over low heat. Add walnuts; cook, stirring occasionally, 5 minutes or until walnuts are lightly toasted. Remove from heat; cool.

When ready to serve, add radishes, olives, cheese and walnuts to chicken mixture; toss until well mixed. Arrange chicken mixture and tomatoes on salad plates lined with greens. Garnish as desired.

Hidden Valley Ranch® Lemon Herb Dressing:
Measure ½ cup *each* extra virgin olive oil and lemon juice, 1 tablespoon light brown sugar and 1 package (1 ounce) Hidden Valley Ranch® Salad Dressing Mix into a glass jar with a tightly fitting lid. Cover and shake until well blended.

*R*oasting and Peeling Peppers

Place peppers on a rack in a broiler pan 3 to 5 inches from heat source, or hold over an open gas flame on the end of a long-handled metal fork. Roast peppers, turning often, until blistered and charred on all sides. Transfer to a plastic bag; seal bag and let stand 15 to 20 minutes to loosen the skins. Remove loosened skins with a paring knife. Cut peppers in half and remove the seeds and stems.

Grilled Chicken, Corn & Avocado Salad

♦ Philippa Farrar from Santa Barbara, California was a finalist at the California Avocado Festival Cook-Off, Carpinteria, California.

Serves 4

2 tablespoons lime juice
2 tablespoons vinegar
1 cup olive oil
1 small bunch cilantro, divided
1 clove garlic, peeled
2 green onions, cut into 1-inch pieces
Salt and black pepper to taste
6 ears fresh corn,* silk and husks intact
2 whole chicken breasts, split and boned
2 Anaheim or poblano peppers,* roasted, peeled and diced
1 large red bell pepper,* roasted, peeled and diced
2 large avocados, peeled, pitted and diced
Crisp salad greens

Pour lime juice and vinegar into food processor or blender container. With processor on, slowly add oil. Add ¾ of the cilantro leaves; process until leaves are finely chopped. Add garlic, green onions, salt and black pepper; process until onions are chopped. Set dressing aside.

Roast corn in husks on covered grill over medium-hot heat about 25 minutes or until tender. Cool slightly, then remove husks and silk. Cut corn from cobs; set aside.

Season chicken with salt and black pepper. Grill or broil skin side 8 minutes. Turn and cook 5 minutes more or until chicken is tender; keep warm.

Toss corn with roasted peppers, avocados and desired amount of dressing in large bowl. Arrange chicken on serving plate lined with greens. Garnish with remaining cilantro. Serve with corn mixture; pass remaining dressing.

*Two cups frozen corn, cooked, 1 can (4 ounces) chopped green chilies, drained, and 1 jar (7 ounces) roasted red peppers, drained, may be substituted for the fresh corn and peppers.

Papaya is a tropical fruit native to the Americas. When ripe, the skin is usually deep yellow. It can be served either raw or cooked. The center of the papaya contains lots of edible black seeds that have a peppery taste. They can be used as a garnish or added to salad dressings. If you make a gelatin mold with papaya, cook the fruit first. Raw papaya contains an enzyme called "papain" and it will prevent the gelatin from setting up properly.

Larry's Pineapple Hula Salad

♦ Larry Grills was the first prize winner in the Salad category in "Generations of Good Cooking," an employee contest sponsored by Dole Packaged Foods Company.

Makes 4 servings

   2 cans (8 ounces each) Dole® Pineapple
       Chunks, drained
   2 cups cubed cooked chicken
   1 cup diagonally sliced celery
   1 cup diced papaya
   ½ cup macadamia nuts or peanuts
   1 cup mayonnaise
   2 teaspoons curry powder
       Crisp salad greens
       Chives and sliced kumquats, for garnish

Combine pineapple, chicken, celery, papaya and nuts in large bowl. Blend mayonnaise and curry powder in small bowl; pour over chicken mixture and blend thoroughly. Cover; refrigerate at least 1 hour. Serve mounded on salad greens. Garnish with chives and kumquats.

Lagoon Chicken Salad

♦ Gloria Kirchman from Minnesota was a prize winner in the National Chicken Cooking Contest, sponsored by the National Broiler Council.

Makes 4 to 6 servings

1½ **cups unsweetened apple juice**
  2 **whole chicken breasts**
  3 **cups cooked rice**
1½ **cups seedless green grapes, halved**
  1 **cup chopped unpeeled apple**
  ½ **cup chopped celery**
  ¾ **cup slivered almonds, divided**
  ½ **cup chopped water chestnuts**
  1 **cup mayonnaise**
  ½ **teaspoon seasoned salt**
  ¼ **teaspoon ground cinnamon**
    Fresh spinach leaves
    Apple slices, for garnish

Bring apple juice to a simmer in deep saucepan over medium heat; add chicken. Cover; simmer about 30 minutes or until tender. Remove chicken from pan; cool. (Reserve broth for another use, if desired.) Remove and discard skin and bones; dice chicken.

Gently toss chicken with rice, grapes, apple, celery, ½ cup of the almonds and the water chestnuts in large bowl. Combine mayonnaise, seasoned salt and cinnamon in small bowl; add to chicken mixture and toss lightly. Cover; refrigerate at least 30 minutes. To serve, spoon chicken mixture onto spinach-lined platter. Sprinkle with remaining ¼ cup almonds; garnish with apple slices.

Montmorency Cherry Chicken Salad

♦ Linda Burke from Williamsville, New York was a finalist in the Cherry Creations Recipe Contest, sponsored by the New York Cherry Growers Association.

Serves 6

> 3 **nectarines or peaches, divided**
> 2 **cups tart red Montmorency cherries, pitted***
> 3 **cups cooked cubed chicken**
> 1½ **cups sliced celery**
> 2 **tablespoons sliced green onions**
> 1 **cup mayonnaise**
> ¼ **cup sour cream**
> 2 **tablespoons honey**
> 1 **teaspoon lemon juice**
> ¼ to ½ **teaspoon curry powder**
> ⅛ **teaspoon ground ginger**
> **Salt to taste**
> ½ **cup toasted slivered almonds, divided**
> **Boston or Bibb lettuce leaves**

Slice 1 of the nectarines; combine with cherries, chicken, celery and green onions in large bowl. Combine mayonnaise, sour cream, honey, lemon juice, curry powder, ginger and salt in small bowl, mixing well. Pour mayonnaise mixture over chicken mixture; toss to coat. Cover; refrigerate until chilled. Just before serving, stir in all but 1 tablespoon of the almonds. Arrange chicken salad on lettuce-lined salad plates. Slice remaining 2 nectarines; garnish with nectarines and almonds.

*Fresh, canned or frozen cherries may be used. Thaw frozen cherries. Drain canned and thawed cherries before using.

Making Mayonnaise

When making mayonnaise, it is essential to add the oil gradually to the egg yolks in order for the mixture to thicken properly. If the oil is added too quickly, the mayonnaise will be runny and the oil will separate from the yolks.

When mixing mayonnaise by hand, start beating in the oil a drop or two at a time until you have incorporated 2 or 3 tablespoons. Then, while beating constantly, begin to add the oil in a thin, steady stream.

When using a food processor or blender, substitute 1 whole egg for the 2 yolks; this makes the mayonnaise more stable and less likely to separate. Turn the machine on and add the oil a teaspoon at a time. After ¼ cup has been added, pour the oil in a thin, steady stream while processing continuously.

Rainbow Chicken Salad

♦ Pamela Stross from Colorado was a prize winner in the National Chicken Cooking Contest, sponsored by the National Broiler Council.

Makes 4 to 6 servings

- 2 **cups water**
- 2 **whole chicken breasts**
- 1 **teaspoon salt**
- ¼ **teaspoon pepper**
  Orange-Mustard Mayonnaise (recipe follows)
- 1 **head romaine lettuce**
- 2 **avocados, peeled, pitted and sliced lengthwise**
- 2 **grapefruit, peeled and sectioned Juice of 1 lemon**
- 4 **navel oranges, peeled and sectioned**
- 1 **red onion, sliced into rings Orange zest, for garnish**

Bring water to a simmer in deep saucepan over medium heat; add chicken, salt and pepper. Cover; simmer about 30 minutes or until tender. While chicken is cooking, prepare Orange-Mustard Mayonnaise. Remove chicken from pan; cool. (Reserve broth for another use, if desired.) Remove and discard skin and bones from chicken; cut into thin slices and set aside.

Arrange lettuce on platter with stalks toward center. Alternately arrange avocados and grapefruit around edge of lettuce; sprinkle with lemon juice. Arrange oranges and onion inside avocados and grapefruit. Arrange chicken in center. Spoon some Orange-Mustard Mayonnaise over chicken; garnish with orange zest. Serve with remaining mayonnaise.

Orange-Mustard Mayonnaise: Beat 2 egg yolks with 2 teaspoons Dijon-style mustard and 1 teaspoon lemon juice in medium-sized bowl. Gradually add 1 cup olive oil, beating in a drop or two at a time with a wire whisk. After 3 tablespoons have been added, pour in a thin, steady stream, beating constantly, until mixture thickens. Stir in grated peel of 1 orange, juice from ½ orange and salt and pepper to taste.

ONE-DISH MEALS

Marinating chicken in a bath of flavorful liquids provides a twofold benefit: it infuses the chicken with a wonderful flavor and also increases its tenderness. Place the chicken in a plastic bag or shallow glass or stainless steel container. Pour the marinade over the chicken; cover and refrigerate for a few minutes, hours or overnight. The longer it marinates, the more flavor it will have. Turn the chicken occasionally so the marinade penetrates evenly.

Chicken Picante

♦ Sally Vog from Oregon was a prize winner in the National Chicken Cooking Contest, sponsored by t National Broiler Council.

Makes 6 servings

½ cup medium-hot chunky taco sauce
¼ cup Dijon-style mustard
2 tablespoons fresh lime juice
3 whole chicken breasts, split, skinned a boned
2 tablespoons butter or margarine
Chopped cilantro, for garnish
Plain yogurt

Combine taco sauce, mustard and lime jui large bowl. Add chicken, turning to coat. C marinate in refrigerator at least 30 minutes

Melt butter in large skillet over medium he foamy. Remove chicken from marinade; re marinade. Add chicken to skillet; cook abo minutes or until brown on both sides. Add marinade; cook about 5 minutes or until ch tender and marinade glazes chicken. Remo chicken to serving platter. Boil marinade o heat 1 minute; pour over chicken. Garnish cilantro. Serve with yogurt.

Baked Chicken Reuben

♦ Marcia Adams from Indiana was a prize win[...]
the National Chicken Cooking Contest, sponso[...]
the National Broiler Council.

Makes 6 to 8 servings

> **4 whole chicken breasts, split, skinned[...]
>   boned**
> ¼ **teaspoon salt**
> ⅛ **teaspoon pepper**
> **1 can (16 ounces) sauerkraut, well drai[...]**
> **4 (6×4-inch) slices Swiss cheese**
> 1¼ **cups Thousand Island salad dressing**

Preheat oven to 325°F. Place chicken in a s[...]
layer in greased baking pan. Sprinkle with [...]
and pepper. Press excess liquid from sauer[...]
spoon over chicken. Arrange cheese slices [...]
sauerkraut. Pour dressing evenly over the t[...]
Cover pan with aluminum foil. Bake about [...]
1½ hours or until chicken is tender.

Sauerkraut is chopped cabbage that has been salted and fermented. It is German in origin and literally means "sour cabbage." This does not mean you should ignore the expiration date on the package. Sauerkraut that has gone sour is not the same thing as cabbage that has been intentionally fermented and salt-pickled.

Green onion brushes make a pretty garnish. Trim roots and most of the green tops from green onions. Make parallel cuts, about 1½ inches long, along the length of each onion at the root end or both ends. Fan out the cuts to form a brush. If desired, place the brushes in a bowl of ice water for several hours so they open and curl.

Chicken Cherry-Yaki Stir-F

♦ Marion C. Boesl from Williamsville, New Yor first place winner in the Cherry Creations Recipe Contest, sponsored by the New York Cherry Grc Association.

Serves 4

1½ cups tart red cherries, pitted (frozen o
    canned)
2 whole chicken breasts, split, skinned boned
2 tablespoons teriyaki sauce
2 tablespoons dry sherry
1 tablespoon lemon juice
3 (¼-inch) slices fresh ginger
1 tablespoon cornstarch
2 to 3 tablespoons peanut or vegetable o
6 green onions, diagonally sliced into
    1-inch pieces
2 small carrots, thinly sliced
2 cups snow peas
4 ounces sliced water chestnuts, drained
2 ounces Chinese rice stick noodles, coo
    2 cups hot cooked rice
¼ cup slivered toasted almonds, for garn
4 green onion brushes, for garnish

Thaw cherries if frozen. Drain cherries, rese juice; set aside. Cut chicken into bite-sized c Combine teriyaki sauce, sherry, lemon juice ginger in small bowl; stir in chicken. Cover; marinate in refrigerator 1 hour, stirring once twice.

Drain chicken, reserving marinade. Discard ginger. Blend reserved cherry juice into cornstarch; stir in marinade and set aside. H tablespoons oil in wok or large skillet over h heat. Add sliced green onions, carrots and sr peas; stir-fry 2 to 3 minutes or until crisp-ter Remove vegetables from wok; add more oil wok, if needed. Add chicken; stir-fry 2 to 3 minutes or until tender. Push chicken away f center of wok; add cornstarch mixture. Cook stir until thickened and bubbly. Stir in chicke cherries, vegetables and water chestnuts; hea through. Serve over noodles. Garnish with almonds and green onion brushes.

Rick's Good-As-Gold Chili

♦ Rick Christman from Mobridge, South Dakot
prize winner at the Golden Chili Pepper Awards,
sponsored by the American Spice Trade Associati

Makes 4½ cups

   ⅓ **cup water**
   ¼ **cup instant minced onion**
   2 **teaspoons instant minced garlic**
   ½ **cup vegetable oil**
   1½ **pounds skinned and boned chicken br**
   1 **can (15 ounces) tomato sauce**
   ¾ **cup beer**
   ½ **cup chicken broth**
   2 **tablespoons chili powder**
   2 **teaspoons ground cumin**
   1 **teaspoon dried oregano, crushed**
   1 **teaspoon soy sauce**
   1 **teaspoon Worcestershire sauce**
   ¾ **teaspoon salt**
   ½ **teaspoon paprika**
   ½ **teaspoon ground red pepper**
   ¼ **teaspoon turmeric**
   ⅛ **teaspoon rubbed sage**
   ⅛ **teaspoon dried thyme, crushed**
   ⅛ **teaspoon dry mustard**

Combine water, onion and garlic in small bo
stand for 10 minutes to soften. Heat oil in la
skillet until hot. Add chicken, a few pieces a
time; cook until golden brown, about 5 min
on each side. Remove and drain on paper to
Cool slightly; cut into ¼-inch cubes and set
Pour off all but 2 tablespoons oil from skille
oil until hot. Add softened onion and garlic;
and stir about 5 minutes or until golden. Ad
remaining ingredients and chicken; mix well
Bring to a boil; reduce heat and simmer abou
minutes, stirring occasionally, until sauce thi
slightly. Garnish as desired.

Chicken Timatar

♦ Raymonde Woodward from Enosburg Falls, V
was the third prize winner in the Delmarva Chic
Cooking Contest, Georgetown, Delaware.

Makes 6 servings

   4 tablespoons vegetable oil
   2 medium-size onions, chopped
   6 cloves garlic, very finely chopped
   4 whole cardamom pods *or* 1/4 teaspoon g
       cardamom
   1 (1-inch) piece fresh ginger, very finely
       chopped
   1 (1-inch) cinnamon stick
   1 teaspoon cumin seeds *or* 1/4 teaspoon gr
       cumin
   1 bay leaf
   6 whole chicken legs (thighs attached),
       skinned
   3 medium-size tomatoes, chopped
   1/2 teaspoon salt
   1/2 teaspoon black pepper
   1/8 teaspoon ground red pepper
   2 tablespoons all-purpose flour
   3 tablespoons water

Heat oil in large skillet or Dutch oven over
medium-high heat. Add onions, garlic,
cardamom, ginger, cinnamon, cumin and ba
Reduce heat to medium; cook and stir 5 minu
Add chicken, tomatoes, salt and black and re
peppers. Bring to a boil, then reduce heat to l
Cover tightly; simmer 30 minutes or until chi
is tender, turning after 15 minutes. Combine
and water; stir into tomato mixture. Cook and
5 minutes or until thickened. Remove cardam
pods, cinnamon stick and bay leaf before ser

Fresh ginger is completely different from dry ginger powder in both appearance and flavor. Resembling a gnarled, tan-colored root, fresh ginger adds its own distinctive pungency and aroma to foods and is used extensively in the dishes of the Far East. Store fresh ginger indefinitely by peeling and cutting it into small chunks. Put it in a glass jar and add enough dry sherry to cover. Store, covered, in the refrigerator.

Ginger Spicy Chicken

♦ Priscilla Yee from Concord, California was the prize winner in the Pace® Picante Sauce 40th Anniversary Recipe Contest, sponsored by Pace Foods, Inc.

Makes 4 servings

    Salt
    2 whole chicken breasts, split, skinned a
        boned
    2 tablespoons vegetable oil
    1 medium-size red bell pepper, cut into
        2×¼-inch strips
    1 medium-size green bell pepper, cut int
        2×¼-inch strips
    1 can (8 ounces) pineapple chunks in jui
        undrained
    ½ cup Pace® picante sauce
    2 tablespoons chopped cilantro or parsle
    2 to 3 teaspoons grated fresh ginger *or*
        ¾ to 1 teaspoon ground ginger

Lightly salt chicken breasts. Heat oil in large skillet over medium heat. Add chicken; cook about 5 minutes on each side or until light b and tender. Remove chicken; keep warm. Ad pepper strips, pineapple, picante sauce, cilar and ginger to skillet. Cook, stirring frequent to 7 minutes or until peppers are tender and is thickened. Return chicken to skillet and he through.

Brown rice is more nutritious than white rice because it contains the bran and germ of the rice kernel. These are removed during milling to produce white rice, which is the staple food for about one-third of the world's population. Converted white rice, however, contains more nutrients than ordinary white rice. It is parboiled before milling, a process that allows some of the vitamins and minerals to be absorbed into the core of the rice kernel.

Lipton® Fried Rice with Chicken

♦ Karen Chasse from Pelham, New Hampshire first place winner in the Senior High category i "Cook America's Heritage" Recipe Contest, spo by Scholastic, Inc. and Lipton® Recipe Soup Mi

Makes about 4 servings

     2 tablespoons vegetable oil, divided
     1 cup chopped bok choy (Chinese cabb
        green cabbage
     1 cup snow peas
     ¼ cup sliced green onions
     1 clove garlic, finely chopped
     1 pound skinned and boned chicken br
        cut into thin strips
     1 envelope Lipton® Onion-Mushroom
        Soup Mix
     ¾ cup water
     1 tablespoon soy sauce
     ⅛ teaspoon pepper
     2 cups cooked brown or white rice (cook
        unsalted water)

Heat 1 tablespoon of the oil in wok or large over medium-high heat. Add bok choy, sno peas, green onions and garlic; stir-fry 3 min until vegetables are crisp-tender. Remove vegetables; reserve. Heat remaining 1 tables oil in wok. Add chicken strips; stir-fry 3 min or until tender. Thoroughly blend soup mix, water, soy sauce and pepper in small bowl; s into chicken. Add cooked rice and vegetable completely through and serve.

Boning a Chicken Breast

1. For easier handling, freeze the chicken until it is firm, but not hard. Remove the skin.

2. For each breast half, use a sharp knife to make three or four arched cuts between the meat and the bone, lifting the meat away with your free hand. (Or, slip your fingers between the meat and the bone and work the meat free without the aid of a knife.)

3. When the meat and bone are separated, remove the heavy white tendon that runs along the length of the breast. This will prevent the meat from shrinking as it cooks.

Chicken Mexicana

♦ Adrienne Sloboden from Puyallup, Washington was the grand prize winner in the Pace® Picante Sauce Young Cooks Recipe Contest, sponsored by Pace Foods, Inc.

Makes 4 servings

    2 whole chicken breasts, split, skinned and
      boned
 ¼ teaspoon garlic salt
    2 tablespoons butter or margarine
 ½ cup sliced green onions with tops
      (½-inch slices)
 ½ cup chopped green bell pepper
    2 to 3 cups hot cooked rice
    1 cup Pace® picante sauce
    4 ounces pasteurized process cheese spread,
      diced
    Additional Pace® picante sauce

Sprinkle chicken with garlic salt. Melt butter in large skillet over medium heat. Add chicken; cook 5 minutes. Turn chicken over; add green onions and green pepper around edge of skillet. Cook 5 minutes more or until chicken is tender. Place rice on serving platter. Remove chicken and vegetables from skillet and arrange over rice; keep warm.

Add 1 cup picante sauce and the cheese spread to skillet. Cook and stir until cheese is melted and sauce is hot. Pour cheese sauce over chicken and vegetables. Garnish as desired. Serve with additional picante sauce.

Commercial poultry seasonings vary widely in flavor, depending on the company that produces them. Many are blends of three or more herbs, including parsley, thyme, sage, rosemary and marjoram.

Apple Curry Chicken

♦ Mary Oatway from Augusta, Maine was a finalist in the Delmarva Chicken Cooking Contest, Georgetown, Delaware.

Makes 4 servings

  2 **whole chicken breasts, split, skinned and boned**
  1 **cup apple juice, divided**
  ¼ **teaspoon salt**
     Dash of pepper
1½ **cups plain croutons**
  1 **medium-size apple, chopped**
  ½ **cup finely chopped onion**
  ¼ **cup raisins**
  2 **teaspoons brown sugar**
  1 **teaspoon curry powder**
  ¾ **teaspoon poultry seasoning**
  ⅛ **teaspoon garlic powder**

Preheat oven to 350°F. Lightly grease shallow baking dish. Arrange chicken breasts in a single layer in prepared pan. Combine ¼ cup of the apple juice, the salt and pepper in small bowl. Brush all of the mixture over chicken. Combine croutons, apple, onion, raisins, sugar, curry powder, poultry seasoning and garlic powder in large bowl. Stir in remaining ¾ cup apple juice; spread over chicken. Cover; bake about 45 minutes or until chicken is tender. Garnish as desired.

Stir-Frying Techniques

Follow these simple steps for successful stir-frying:

1. Prepare all the ingredients in advance, including cleaning, cutting, measuring and combining.

2. Cut the meat and vegetables into uniform sizes and shapes to ensure even cooking.

3. Make sure the oil is hot before adding any food to the pan. (The best oils to use for stir-frying are peanut, corn and soybean oils.)

4. Keep the food in constant motion, tossing and stirring it with a flat metal or wooden spatula. This prevents it from burning and also seals in the flavor.

Stir-Fried Chicken

♦ Hope Boyd from McAlester, Oklahoma was a prize winner at the A-OK Cook-Off, sponsored by various Oklahoma agricultural organizations, Oklahoma City, Oklahoma.

Makes about 6 servings

2 whole chicken breasts, split, skinned and boned
2 tablespoons vegetable oil
1 cup diagonally sliced celery
1 medium-size carrot, diagonally sliced
1 medium-size green bell pepper, cut into thin strips
1 cup sliced mushrooms
½ small onion, thinly sliced
1 teaspoon salt
¼ teaspoon ground ginger
1 can (16 ounces) bean sprouts, drained
1 can (5 ounces) water chestnuts, drained and sliced
¼ cup water
2 teaspoons cornstarch
2 tablespoons soy sauce
3 cups hot cooked rice
¾ cup peanuts

Slice chicken crosswise into ¼-inch strips. Heat oil in wok or large skillet over high heat. Add celery, carrot, green pepper, mushrooms, onion, salt and ginger. Stir-fry about 3 minutes or until vegetables are crisp-tender; remove from wok and keep warm. Add chicken to wok; stir-fry 3 to 5 minutes or until tender. Return vegetables to wok; stir in bean sprouts, water chestnuts and water. Blend cornstarch with soy sauce until smooth, then gradually stir into chicken and vegetables. Cook, stirring constantly, until thickened. Mound rice onto serving platter; spoon chicken and vegetables over rice. Sprinkle with peanuts; serve immediately.

Chicken with Lime Butter

♦ Karen Johnson from Kansas was a prize winner in the National Chicken Cooking Contest, sponsored by the National Broiler Council.

Makes 6 servings

> 3 **whole chicken breasts, split, skinned and boned**
> ½ **teaspoon salt**
> ½ **teaspoon pepper**
> ⅓ **cup vegetable oil**
>   **Juice of 1 lime**
> ½ **cup butter**
> 1 **teaspoon minced chives**
> ½ **teaspoon dill weed**

Sprinkle chicken with salt and pepper. Heat oil in large skillet over medium heat. Add chicken; cook until light brown, about 3 minutes per side. Cover; reduce heat to low. Cook 10 minutes or until chicken is tender. Remove chicken to serving platter; keep warm.

Discard oil from skillet. Add lime juice; cook over low heat until juice begins to bubble, about 1 minute. Add butter, 1 tablespoon at a time, stirring until butter becomes opaque and forms a thickened sauce. Remove from heat; stir in chives and dill weed. Spoon sauce over chicken; serve immediately. Garnish as desired.

Contestants at the Delmarva Chicken Cooking Contest come not only from Delaware, Maryland and Virginia (the vast area that gave the competition its DEL-MAR-VA name), but from all over the country. They are lured by the big prize money and the publicity that always surrounds one of the largest of the food festivals.

Olympic Seoul Chicken

♦ Muriel Brody from Cumberland, Rhode Island was the first prize winner in the Delmarva Chicken Cooking Contest, Georgetown, Delaware.

Serves 4

- ¼ cup white vinegar
- 3 tablespoons soy sauce
- 2 tablespoons honey
- ¼ teaspoon ground ginger
- 2 tablespoons peanut oil
- 8 chicken thighs, skinned
- 10 cloves garlic, coarsely chopped
- ½ to 1 teaspoon crushed red pepper
- 2 ounces Chinese rice stick noodles, cooked *or*
  2 cups hot cooked rice

Combine vinegar, soy sauce, honey and ginger in small bowl; set aside. Heat oil in large skillet over medium-high heat. Add chicken; cook about 10 minutes or until evenly browned on both sides. Add garlic and red pepper; cook, stirring, 2 to 3 minutes. Drain off excess fat. Add vinegar mixture. Cover; reduce heat and simmer about 15 minutes or until chicken is tender. Uncover and cook about 2 minutes or until sauce has reduced and thickened. Serve with noodles and desired vegetables.

Forty-Clove Chicken Filice

♦ Val Filice from Gilroy, California was a finalist in the Gilroy Garlic Festival Recipe Contest, Gilroy, California. Courtesy of the Gilroy Garlic Festival Association's *Garlic Lover's Cookbook.*

Makes 4 to 6 servings

      1 (3-pound) frying chicken, cut into serving
         pieces
     40 cloves fresh garlic, peeled* and left whole
      ½ cup dry white wine
      ¼ cup dry vermouth
      ¼ cup olive oil
      4 ribs celery, thickly sliced
      2 tablespoons finely chopped parsley
      2 teaspoons dried basil
      1 teaspoon dried oregano
         Pinch of crushed red pepper
      1 lemon
         Salt and black pepper to taste

Preheat oven to 375°F. Place chicken pieces, skin side up, in a single layer in shallow baking pan. Combine garlic, wine, vermouth, oil, celery, parsley, basil, oregano and red pepper in medium-sized bowl; mix thoroughly. Sprinkle garlic mixture over chicken pieces. Remove zest from lemon in thin strips; place zest throughout pan. Squeeze juice from lemon and pour over the top. Season with salt and black pepper. Cover pan with aluminum foil. Bake 40 minutes. Remove foil and bake another 15 minutes. Garnish as desired.

See page 6 for helpful tips on peeling garlic.

SAVORY SUPPERS

Always use tongs to turn chicken pieces over during cooking. This prevents the skin from being pierced, keeping the natural juices sealed inside the skin.

Bittersweet Farm Chicken

♦ Ann Combs from New Hampshire was a prize winner in the National Chicken Cooking Contest, sponsored by the National Broiler Council.

Makes 4 servings

½ **cup all-purpose flour**
1 **teaspoon salt**
¼ **teaspoon pepper**
1 **(3½- to 4-pound) frying chicken, cut into serving pieces**
8 **tablespoons butter or margarine, divided**
¼ **cup lemon juice**
¼ **cup orange-flavored liqueur**
¼ **cup honey**
2 **tablespoons orange zest**
1 **tablespoon soy sauce**
  Whole cooked baby carrots

Preheat oven to 350°F. Combine flour, salt and pepper in large plastic bag. Add chicken pieces, a few at a time, to bag; shake to coat completely with flour mixture. Melt 4 tablespoons of the butter in large baking pan. Roll chicken in butter to coat all sides; arrange skin side down in a single layer in pan. Bake 30 minutes.

Meanwhile, melt remaining 4 tablespoons butter in small saucepan over medium heat. Stir in lemon juice, liqueur, honey, orange zest and soy sauce; reserve 2 tablespoons of the mixture. Remove chicken from oven; turn pieces over. Pour remaining honey mixture over chicken. Continue baking, basting occasionally, 30 minutes or until chicken is glazed and tender. Toss reserved honey mixture with cooked carrots; serve with chicken. Garnish as desired.

Apricot Chicken Oriental

♦ Harriet Kuhn of Patterson, California was a prize winner in the Apricot Sweepstakes at the Patterson Apricot Fiesta, sponsored by the Apricot Advisory Board, Walnut Creek, California.

Makes 4 servings

   1 tablespoon butter or margarine
   2 whole chicken breasts, split, skinned and boned
   1 jar (10 ounces) apricot preserves
   1 cup water
   ½ cup soy sauce
   1 can (8 ounces) sliced water chestnuts, drained and liquid reserved
  12 dried apricots, coarsely chopped
   1 teaspoon ground ginger
   1 teaspoon garlic powder
     Apricot Rice (recipe follows)
   3 ribs celery, diagonally sliced
   2 cups sliced mushrooms
   1 bunch green onions, sliced
   1 package (6 ounces) frozen pea pods
   1 red or green bell pepper, cut into strips

Melt butter in large skillet over medium heat. Add chicken; cook until brown on both sides. Stir in preserves, water, soy sauce, liquid from water chestnuts, apricots, ginger and garlic powder. Simmer 40 minutes or until chicken is tender. Meanwhile, prepare Apricot Rice. Add celery, mushrooms, green onions, pea pods, red pepper and water chestnuts to skillet; cook and stir 5 minutes or until heated through. Serve chicken and vegetables over rice. Garnish as desired.

Apricot Rice: Combine 2½ cups water, ¼ cup finely chopped dried apricots and ¼ teaspoon salt in medium-sized saucepan. Bring to a boil; stir in 1 cup long-grain rice. Cover; reduce heat and simmer 20 minutes. Remove from heat; let stand 5 minutes.

If you buy an avocado that is not fully ripe, put it in a brown paper bag and keep it at room temperature. It will soften within a day or two. When you are ready to eat it, cut it with a stainless steel knife and sprinkle it with lemon or lime juice; this will prevent it from discoloring.

Hot Stuffed Avocados with Creamed Chicken

♦ David Sledd of New Orleans, Louisiana was the winner in the Poultry category of *The Times Picayune* Cookbook Recipe Contest.

Serves 6

6 tablespoons lime juice
6 cloves garlic, peeled
3 ripe avocados, halved and pitted
3 tablespoons butter or margarine
3 tablespoons all-purpose flour
1 cup heavy cream
2 cups diced cooked chicken
1½ tablespoons grated onion
¼ teaspoon celery salt
    Salt and pepper to taste
½ cup (2 ounces) shredded sharp Cheddar cheese
    Snipped chives, for garnish

Place 1 tablespoon lime juice and 1 clove garlic in each avocado half. Let stand at room temperature 30 minutes.

Preheat oven to 350°F. Melt butter in large skillet over low heat; blend in flour. Gradually stir in cream; cook, stirring constantly, until thickened. Stir in chicken, onion, celery salt, salt and pepper. Discard lime juice and garlic from avocados. Fill avocados with chicken mixture; sprinkle with cheese. Arrange in a single layer in baking dish. Pour water into dish to a depth of ½ inch. Bake 15 minutes or until cheese melts. Garnish with chives.

Curry powder is formed by blending together a number of spices, including turmeric, cardamom, cumin, pepper, cloves, cinnamon, nutmeg and sometimes ginger. Chilies give it heat and ground dried garlic provides depth of taste. Curry blends vary depending on their use. Milder powders are used for fish and eggs; stronger ones season meats and poultry. There are also regional variations. Store curry powder away from the heat of the stove to preserve its full strength and pungency.

Curried Chicken Rolls

♦ Barbara Long from Wyoming was a prize winner in the National Chicken Cooking Contest, sponsored by the National Broiler Council.

Makes 4 servings

  2 **whole chicken breasts, split, skinned and boned**
½ **teaspoon salt**
⅛ **teaspoon pepper**
  1 **tablespoon butter or margarine**
½ **medium-size onion, finely chopped**
¾ **cup cooked rice**
¼ **cup raisins**
  1 **tablespoon chopped parsley**
  1 **teaspoon curry powder**
  1 **teaspoon brown sugar**
½ **teaspoon poultry seasoning**
    Pinch of garlic powder
  1 **tablespoon vegetable oil**
½ **cup dry white wine**
  1 **teaspoon instant chicken bouillon granules**

Pound chicken breasts between 2 pieces of plastic wrap to ⅜-inch thickness; sprinkle with salt and pepper. Melt butter in medium-sized skillet over medium heat. Add onion; cook and stir about 3 minutes or until soft. Remove from heat. Add rice, raisins, parsley, curry powder, brown sugar, poultry seasoning and garlic powder; mix well. Divide rice mixture into 4 equal portions. Spoon 1 portion onto each chicken breast. Roll up chicken jelly-roll fashion; secure with wooden toothpicks. Heat oil in large skillet over medium heat; add chicken rolls. Cook about 15 minutes or until brown on all sides. Add wine and bouillon. Cover; simmer 30 minutes or until chicken is tender. Garnish as desired.

Serving Suggestion: Additional rice stuffing may be prepared and served alongside the chicken rolls. Bake the extra stuffing in a covered casserole at 350°F until heated through.

Fresh Gazpacho Chicken

♦ Gloria Piantek from Skillman, New Jersey was a second prize winner in the Delmarva Chicken Cooking Contest, Georgetown, Delaware.

Makes 4 servings

¼ **cup all-purpose flour**
1½ **teaspoons salt, divided**
½ **teaspoon paprika**
¼ **teaspoon black pepper, divided**
2 **whole chicken breasts, split**
¼ **cup vegetable oil**
2½ **cups tomato juice**
½ **cup finely chopped, seeded tomatoes**
½ **cup finely chopped carrots**
½ **cup finely chopped celery**
½ **cup finely chopped onion**
½ **cup finely chopped green pepper**
½ **cup finely chopped, peeled, seeded cucumber**
½ **cup red wine vinegar**
¼ **cup olive oil**
5 **teaspoons Worcestershire sauce**
5 **dashes hot pepper sauce**
2 **cloves garlic, crushed**
Hot cooked rice

Combine flour, 1 teaspoon of the salt, the paprika and ⅛ teaspoon of the black pepper in shallow dish. Add chicken, one piece at a time, dredging to coat. Heat vegetable oil in large skillet over medium heat; add chicken. Cook about 10 minutes or until brown on both sides; drain off oil. Combine remaining ingredients, *except* rice, in large bowl. Stir in remaining ½ teaspoon salt and ⅛ teaspoon black pepper. Reserve 1 cup of the tomato mixture; cover and refrigerate. Pour remaining tomato mixture over chicken in skillet. Cover; cook over medium heat, turning occasionally, about 30 minutes or until chicken is tender. Arrange chicken on serving platter; spoon about 1 cup pan juices over chicken. Serve with chilled tomato mixture and rice. Garnish as desired.

A member of the parsley family, dill weed is the dried soft feathery leaves of the dill plant. Dill is the cornerstone of Scandinavian cooking, where it turns up in everything from scrambled eggs to fish, cucumbers and sandwiches. Central European and Russian cooks also prefer it above other herbs. Its distinctive flavor can easily dominate a dish so you may want to use it sparingly at first.

Calorie-Wise Dill Chicken

♦ Anna Bodisch from Coplay, Pennsylvania was a finalist in the National Chicken Cooking Contest, sponsored by the National Broiler Council.

Makes 4 servings

    1 cup plain low-fat yogurt
1½ cups regular wheat germ
  ½ cup chopped almonds
    2 teaspoons dried dill weed
  ½ teaspoon salt
  ¼ teaspoon pepper
12 chicken drumsticks
    Nonstick vegetable cooking spray

Preheat oven to 350°F. Place yogurt in shallow bowl. Combine wheat germ, almonds, dill weed, salt and pepper in another shallow bowl. Dip chicken drumsticks, one at a time, into yogurt, then roll in wheat germ mixture to coat. Line baking sheet with aluminum foil; spray with nonstick vegetable cooking spray. Arrange chicken in a single layer on baking sheet. Bake about 50 minutes or until chicken is tender. Garnish as desired.

Chicken Avocado Melt

♦ Marjorie Fortier from Connecticut was a prize winner in the National Chicken Cooking Contest, sponsored by the National Broiler Council.

Makes 4 servings

2 whole chicken breasts, split, skinned and boned
2 tablespoons cornstarch
1 teaspoon ground cumin
1 teaspoon garlic salt
1 egg, slightly beaten
1 tablespoon water
⅓ cup yellow cornmeal
3 tablespoons vegetable oil
1 firm ripe avocado, peeled and sliced
1½ cups (6 ounces) shredded Monterey Jack cheese
½ cup sour cream
¼ cup sliced green onion tops
¼ cup chopped red bell pepper

Preheat oven to 350°F. Pound chicken breasts between 2 pieces of plastic wrap to ¼-inch thickness. Combine cornstarch, cumin and garlic salt in shallow dish. Add chicken, dredging to coat. Combine egg and water in small bowl. Place cornmeal in shallow dish. Dip chicken into egg mixture, then roll in cornmeal to coat. Heat oil in large skillet over medium heat. Add chicken; cook 2 minutes on each side. Remove chicken to shallow baking pan. Arrange avocado slices over chicken; sprinkle with cheese. Bake about 15 minutes or until chicken is tender and cheese melts. Transfer chicken to serving platter. Top with sour cream; sprinkle with green onions and red pepper.

Chicken in Lemon Sauce

♦ Nelda Smith from Oklahoma was a prize winner in the National Chicken Cooking Contest, sponsored by the National Broiler Council.

Makes 8 servings

- ¼ **cup butter or margarine**
- 4 **whole chicken breasts, split, skinned and boned**
- 2 **tablespoons dry white wine**
- ½ **teaspoon grated lemon peel**
- 2 **tablespoons lemon juice**
- ¼ **teaspoon salt**
- ⅛ **teaspoon white pepper**
- 1 **cup heavy cream**
- ⅓ **cup grated Parmesan cheese**
- 1 **cup sliced mushrooms**
  Red grapes and lemon peel, for garnish

Melt butter in large skillet over medium heat; add chicken. Cook, turning, about 10 minutes or until chicken is brown and tender. Remove chicken to ovenproof serving dish. Discard butter from skillet. Add wine, lemon peel and lemon juice to skillet; cook and stir over medium heat 1 minute. Stir in salt and white pepper. Gradually pour in cream, stirring constantly, until hot; *do not boil*. Pour cream sauce over chicken; sprinkle with cheese and mushrooms. Broil chicken about 6 inches from heat source until lightly browned. Garnish with grapes and lemon peel.

Pounding boned chicken breasts to a uniform thickness, usually 1/4 inch, allows them to cook faster and more evenly. It also flattens them so that a savory filling can be rolled up inside. Place the chicken between two pieces of plastic wrap to prevent it from tearing. Using the flat bottom (not the edge) of a meat pounder or a rolling pin, pound the chicken with a downward motion until it is evenly flattened.

Laguna Beach Pecan Chicken

♦ Carol Miller from Gansevoort, New York was a finalist in the Hidden Valley Ranch®/California Ripe Olive "Tastes of the West" Cooking Contest, sponsored by the California Olive Industry, Fresno, California.

Makes 8 servings

> 4 whole chicken breasts, split, skinned and boned
> Pepper to taste
> 6 tablespoons unsalted butter or vegetable oil
> 1/4 cup plus 2 tablespoons Dijon-style mustard, divided
> 2 cups pecan halves, finely ground
> 1 1/2 to 2 cups plain yogurt
> 1 cup California ripe olives, sliced
> 1 package (1 ounce) Hidden Valley Ranch® Original Ranch® Salad Dressing Mix

Preheat oven to 400°F. Pound chicken breasts between 2 pieces of plastic wrap to 1/4-inch thickness; sprinkle with pepper. Melt butter in small saucepan over low heat. Remove pan from heat; whisk in 1/4 cup of the mustard. (If using oil, whisk oil with 1/4 cup mustard in small bowl.) Dip chicken into mustard mixture, then roll in ground pecans to coat. Arrange chicken in a single layer in lightly greased baking pan. Bake 15 minutes or until golden and tender.

Meanwhile, thoroughly combine yogurt, olives, salad dressing mix and remaining 2 tablespoons mustard in medium-sized saucepan. Remove chicken from pan. Stir pan drippings into yogurt mixture; simmer over low heat 2 minutes. Place 2 tablespoons yogurt sauce on each dinner plate; top with a chicken breast. Serve with remaining sauce.

COME FOR DINNER

If you skin and debone your own chicken breasts, be sure to reserve both the bones and skin. Let these scraps collect in a plastic bag in your freezer and soon you'll have enough to make flavorful homemade chicken stock.

Curried Chicken Calcutta

♦ Alice Cory from King of Prussia, Pennsylvania won honorable mention in the Delmarva Chicken Cooking Contest, Georgetown, Delaware.

Makes 4 servings

¼ **cup all-purpose flour**
½ **teaspoon curry powder**
½ **teaspoon ground cinnamon**
½ **teaspoon ground ginger**
¼ **teaspoon garlic powder**
2 **whole chicken breasts, split, skinned and boned**
¼ **cup vegetable oil**
1 **cup plain yogurt**
2 **tablespoons lime juice**
 Peel of 1 lime, grated
 Lime slices and mint sprigs, for garnish

Combine flour, curry powder, cinnamon, ginger and garlic powder in shallow dish. Add chicken, one piece at a time, dredging to coat. Heat oil in large skillet over medium heat. Add chicken; cook until brown on both sides. Cover; reduce heat to low and cook 15 minutes or until chicken is tender.

Combine yogurt and lime juice in small saucepan. Cook over low heat, stirring constantly, until warm. Arrange chicken on serving platter. Spoon about one half of the yogurt sauce over chicken; sprinkle with grated lime peel and garnish with lime slices and mint. Pass remaining sauce.

ℋere is a valuable tip to keep in mind in case you should find yourself dying of thirst on a desert island: Eat a cucumber. It is 96 percent water and maintains a lower temperature than the air around it. In fact, it was to have a year-round supply of cucumbers that hothouses were first built.

Chicken with Cucumbers and Dill

♦ Frank Mullin from Washington, D.C. was a third prize winner in the Delmarva Chicken Cooking Contest, Georgetown, Delaware.

Makes 4 servings

　2 whole chicken breasts, split, skinned and boned
　1 teaspoon salt, divided
　¾ teaspoon pepper, divided
　4 tablespoons butter or margarine, divided
　2 cucumbers, peeled, seeded and cut into ¼-inch slices
　½ teaspoon dill weed
　¼ cup lemon juice
　Lemon slices, for garnish

Sprinkle chicken breasts with ½ teaspoon of the salt and ½ teaspoon of the pepper. Melt 2 tablespoons of the butter in large skillet over medium heat; add chicken. Cook about 8 minutes or until chicken is brown on both sides; remove and keep warm. Melt remaining 2 tablespoons butter in same skillet. Add cucumbers; stir to coat. Sprinkle remaining ½ teaspoon salt and ¼ teaspoon pepper over cucumbers; cook 2 minutes. Stir in dill weed. Push cucumbers to side of skillet.

Return chicken and any collected juices to skillet. Cook 2 minutes or until chicken is tender. Place chicken on serving platter; arrange cucumbers around chicken. Cook juices in skillet until light brown. Pour lemon juice and pan juices over chicken. Garnish with lemon slices.

Mustard is one of the most frequently eaten condiments in the world. Although it has been around since the beginning of time, it is only recently that we have begun to glimpse the infinite number of varieties that are available. Dijon mustard is smooth and piquant with a slightly hot undertone and is made in Dijon, France. Dijon-style mustard is its American counterpart. Chinese mustard is more pungent than Dijon and can be so fiery hot that it will bring tears to your eyes if eaten in large amounts. German mustard is milder, sweeter and darker than Dijon or Chinese mustards— the perfect accompaniment to a good sausage.

Chicken with Fruit and Mixed Mustards

♦ Marjorie Farr from Rockville, Maryland was second prize winner in the Delmarva Chicken Cooking Contest, Georgetown, Delaware.

Makes 4 servings

 ½ cup Dijon-style mustard
 ½ cup Bavarian or other German mustard
 1 tablespoon Chinese mustard
 ⅓ cup honey
 ⅓ cup light cream
 2 whole chicken breasts, split, skinned and
    boned
 ½ teaspoon salt
 ¼ teaspoon pepper
 2 tablespoons butter or margarine
 4 kiwifruit, peeled and sliced
 2 cups melon balls (honeydew and
    cantaloupe)
 ¼ cup mayonnaise
   Mint sprigs, for garnish

Combine mustards, honey and cream in medium-sized bowl. Spoon half of the mustard sauce into large glass bowl; reserve remainder. Sprinkle chicken with salt and pepper; place in glass bowl, turning to coat with mustard sauce. Cover; marinate in refrigerator 30 minutes, turning often.

Heat butter in large skillet over medium heat until foamy. Add chicken; cook about 7 minutes on each side or until brown and tender. Remove chicken to cutting board and cut across the grain into thin slices. Arrange chicken and fruit on serving platter.

Place reserved mustard sauce in small saucepan; whisk in mayonnaise. Heat thoroughly over medium heat. Drizzle some sauce over chicken. Garnish platter with mint sprigs. Pass remaining sauce.

Plum Sweet and Spicy Chicken

♦ Joan McCormick from Virginia was a prize winner in the National Chicken Cooking Contest, sponsored by the National Broiler Council.

Makes 4 servings

- ½ teaspoon white pepper
- ½ teaspoon ground ginger
- ½ teaspoon ground cinnamon
- ¼ teaspoon ground cloves
- 1 (3½- to 4-pound) frying chicken
- 4 tablespoons soy sauce, divided
- 2 tablespoons honey
- ½ cup plum jelly
- ¼ cup chutney
- 2 teaspoons sugar
- 2 teaspoons vinegar

Combine white pepper, ginger, cinnamon and cloves in small dish. Rub inside of chicken with half of the spice mixture. Stir 1 tablespoon of the soy sauce into remaining spice mixture; rub on outside of chicken. Cover chicken; refrigerate 1 hour.

Place chicken, breast side up, on rack in wok over 2 inches of boiling water. Cover; steam 1 hour, adding water to wok as needed.

Preheat oven to 350°F. Remove chicken to shallow baking pan. Bake about 15 minutes or until leg moves freely when twisted; remove from oven. *Increase oven temperature to 450°F.* Combine remaining 3 tablespoons soy sauce and the honey; brush on chicken. Combine plum jelly, chutney, sugar and vinegar; spread on chicken. Bake 10 minutes longer or until brown and tender. Let chicken stand 15 minutes before carving. Garnish as desired.

Cream of coconut is made by pressing the white meat of tree-ripened coconuts into a thick liquid. The liquid is then processed into a creamy consistency. It is available in supermarkets in the beverage, baking or specialty foods sections.

Coconut Chicken with Fresh Chutney

♦ Lonnie Gandara from San Francisco, California was second prize winner in the Savory category of the International Association of Cooking Professionals Recipe Contest, sponsored by Coco Lopez® Cream of Coconut, a product of Borden, Inc.

Makes 4 servings

- 1 can (15 ounces) cream of coconut, divided
- 2 tablespoons soy sauce
- 2 whole chicken breasts, split *or* 8 chicken thighs
- 3 cups chopped nectarines or apples
- ½ cup raisins
- ½ lemon, seeded and chopped (about ¼ cup)
- ⅓ cup packed light brown sugar
- ¼ cup cider vinegar
- 1 tablespoon finely chopped fresh ginger
- ½ teaspoon curry powder
- 1 clove garlic, finely chopped
- ¼ cup flaked coconut

Combine ¾ cup of the cream of coconut and the soy sauce. Arrange chicken pieces in 12×7-inch baking dish; pour coconut mixture over the top. Cover; refrigerate overnight, turning occasionally.

Meanwhile, combine nectarines, raisins, lemon, sugar, vinegar, ginger, curry powder and garlic in medium-sized saucepan; mix well. Bring to a boil; boil 2 minutes, stirring occasionally; cool. Add flaked coconut and remaining cream of coconut; mix well. Cover chutney mixture; refrigerate overnight to allow flavors to blend.

Preheat oven to 350°F. Remove chicken from refrigerator; uncover dish. Bake chicken 45 minutes to 1 hour or until tender, basting frequently with coconut marinade. Serve chicken with chutney on the side. Garnish as desired.

Greek-Style Chicken in Filo

♦ Anne Marie Strauss from Coram, New York was first place winner in the Polly-O® International Recipe Competition, sponsored by Pollio Dairy Products Corporation.

Serves 6

3 whole chicken breasts, split, skinned and
   boned
2 tablespoons vegetable oil
¼ cup butter or margarine
1 large onion, chopped
1 can (4 ounces) sliced mushrooms, drained
2 tablespoons parsley flakes
1½ tablespoons finely chopped fresh dill
1 clove garlic, minced
1 package (10 ounces) frozen chopped spinach,
   cooked and drained
1½ tablespoons all-purpose flour
⅓ cup vermouth
1 cup (8 ounces) Polly-O® ricotta cheese
   Salt and pepper to taste
½ cup melted butter or margarine
12 sheets filo dough
   Dry bread crumbs

Pound chicken breasts between 2 pieces of plastic wrap to ¼-inch thickness. Heat oil in large skillet over medium heat. Add chicken; cook until brown on both sides. Remove; drain on paper towels and set aside. Wipe out skillet.

Melt ¼ cup butter in same skillet over medium heat. Add onion; cook and stir until golden. Add mushrooms, parsley flakes, dill, garlic and spinach; cook and stir 2 minutes. Stir in flour, mixing well. Gradually stir in vermouth; cook, stirring constantly, until thickened. Stir in ricotta, salt and pepper; remove from heat.

Preheat oven to 350°F. Brush melted butter on 1 filo sheet; sprinkle with bread crumbs. Cover with another sheet; brush with butter. Place chicken breast in center of filo; spoon ⅙ of the spinach mixture on top. Fold filo over chicken, turning ends under. Repeat for each chicken breast. Place in a single layer in greased baking pan. Brush tops with butter. Bake for 45 minutes or until brown.

Filo dough is of Middle Eastern origin and used to make such classic Greek dishes as spanakopita and baklava. Made of flour and water, it is essentially the same as strudel dough. Long ago it was believed that a bride-to-be was not fit for marriage until she was able to roll filo dough so thinly that her chosen groom would be able, without difficulty, to read the newspaper through it.

Sun-dried tomatoes are a new addition to many supermarket produce departments. Looking much like reddish-brown pieces of dried leather, these chewy tomatoes have a sweet taste and add a rich tomato flavor to soups, stews and sauces. They are also a great garnish for pizza, salads and sandwiches. Sun-dried tomatoes are available in bags or packed in olive oil. Most brands add quite a bit of salt during processing, so use them sparingly.

Chicken Breasts Sautéed with Sun-Dried Tomatoes

♦ Thomas Nobile from Glen Head, New York was first place winner in the Polly-O® Italian Cheese Recipe Contest, sponsored by Pollio Dairy Products Corporation.

Makes 8 servings

   4 whole chicken breasts, split, skinned and boned
   8 to 10 pieces sun-dried tomatoes
   1 container (15 ounces) Polly-O® ricotta cheese
   1 package (4 ounces) Polly-O® shredded mozzarella cheese (1 cup)
   ⅓ cup Polly-O® grated Parmesan or Romano cheese
   1 egg, beaten
   2 tablespoons chopped parsley
   ½ teaspoon garlic powder
   ¼ teaspoon pepper
   2 tablespoons pine nuts
   2 tablespoons currants
   ⅓ cup butter or margarine
   ⅔ cup sliced shallots
   1 cup chicken broth
   ½ cup dry white wine

Pound chicken breasts between 2 pieces of plastic wrap to ¼-inch thickness. Chop enough tomatoes to measure ⅓ cup; slice remaining tomatoes into strips. Combine cheeses, egg, chopped tomatoes, parsley, garlic powder and pepper in medium-sized bowl; blend well. Divide cheese mixture evenly between chicken breasts; spread to within 1 inch of edges. Sprinkle with pine nuts and currants. Roll up chicken jelly-roll fashion; secure with wooden toothpicks, making sure filling is entirely enclosed.

Melt butter in large skillet over medium-high heat; add chicken rolls. Cook until golden on all sides; remove and keep warm. Add shallots and tomato strips to skillet; cook and stir over low heat 2 minutes. Blend in broth and wine; cook 3 minutes. Return chicken to skillet. Cover; simmer 15 to 20 minutes or until tender, basting several times and turning once. Garnish as desired.

Stuffed Chicken with Apple Glaze

♦ Ruth Dykes from Beltsville, Maryland was a first prize winner in the Delmarva Chicken Cooking Contest, Georgetown, Delaware.

Makes 4 servings

1 (3½- to 4-pound) frying chicken
½ teaspoon salt
¼ teaspoon pepper
2 tablespoons vegetable oil
1 package (6 ounces) chicken-flavored stuffing mix, plus ingredients to prepare mix
1 cup chopped apple
¼ cup chopped walnuts
¼ cup raisins
¼ cup thinly sliced celery
½ teaspoon grated lemon peel
½ cup apple jelly
1 tablespoon lemon juice
½ teaspoon ground cinnamon

Preheat oven to 350°F. Sprinkle inside of chicken with salt and pepper; rub outside with oil. Prepare stuffing mix according to package directions in large bowl. Add apple, walnuts, raisins, celery and lemon peel; mix thoroughly. Stuff body cavity loosely with stuffing.* Place chicken in baking pan; cover loosely with aluminum foil and roast 1 hour.

Meanwhile, combine jelly, lemon juice and cinnamon in small saucepan. Simmer over low heat 3 minutes or until blended. Remove foil from chicken; brush with jelly mixture. Roast, uncovered, brushing frequently with jelly glaze, 30 minutes or until meat thermometer inserted into thickest part of thigh registers 185°F. Let chicken stand 15 minutes before carving.

Bake any leftover stuffing in a covered casserole alongside chicken until heated through.

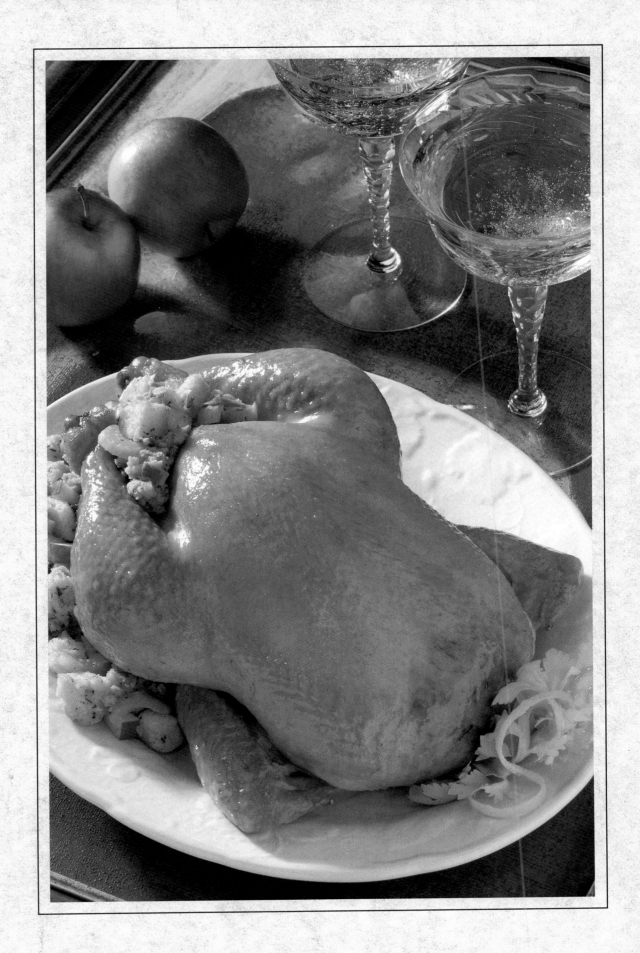

Roast Chicken & Kiwi with Raspberry Glaze

♦ Stephen Abel from Rehoboth Beach, Delaware was a first prize winner in the Delmarva Chicken Cooking Contest, Georgetown, Delaware.

Makes 4 servings

> **2 (3½- to 4-pound) frying chickens, cut into halves**
> **1 teaspoon salt**
> **¼ teaspoon pepper**
> **½ cup butter or margarine, melted**
>   **Raspberry Glaze (recipe follows)**
>   **Kiwifruit, peeled and sliced**

Preheat oven to 400°F. Sprinkle chicken with salt and pepper. Place, skin side up, in a single layer in large shallow pan; brush with butter. Roast, basting frequently with butter, about 45 minutes or until chicken is tender. Drain off fat. While chicken is cooking, prepare Raspberry Glaze. Spoon glaze over chicken; top with kiwi slices. Spoon glaze from bottom of pan over chicken and kiwi. Bake about 3 minutes or until kiwi and chicken are well glazed.

Raspberry Glaze: Combine 1 cup seedless raspberry preserves, ½ cup white port wine and grated peel of 1 lemon in small saucepan. Cook over low heat about 5 minutes or until slightly thick.

Cranberries are a native North American food. Pilgrims noticed that the cranes flew to the cranberry bogs in great flocks and feasted on the sour red berries. Thus they got their name—not craneberries but cranberries.

Cranberry Chicken

♦ Paul Morse was American Regional Cuisine Award winner at the March of Dimes Gourmet Gala in Boston, Massachusetts.

Serves 6

 ⅓ cup vegetable oil
 3 cloves garlic, finely chopped
 3 whole chicken breasts, split
   Salt and black pepper to taste
 2 medium-size green bell peppers, sliced into
   strips
 3 medium-size onions, sliced
 10 large mushrooms, sliced
 ½ cup cider vinegar
 1 can (16 ounces) whole cranberry sauce
 1 cup orange juice
 1 tablespoon cornstarch
 1 tablespoon soy sauce
   Hot cooked rice
   Orange slices and parsley sprigs, for garnish

Heat oil in large skillet over medium-high heat. Add garlic and chicken breasts; cook until chicken is brown on both sides. Season with salt and black pepper. Remove chicken; set aside. Add green peppers, onions and mushrooms to skillet; cook and stir until vegetables are softened. Stir in vinegar, cranberry sauce and orange juice. Add chicken; cook 30 minutes or until chicken is tender. Remove chicken; keep warm.

Combine cornstarch and soy sauce with enough water to make a smooth paste; add to sauce and vegetables. Stir gently over low heat until thickened. Arrange rice and chicken on serving platter. Pour sauce over chicken. Garnish with orange slices and parsley sprigs.

Spinach-Stuffed Chicken

♦ Yvette Jemison from Mandeville, Louisiana was the winner in the Poultry category of *The Times Picayune Cookbook* Recipe Contest.

Makes 4 servings

   2 whole chicken breasts, split and boned
   2 cups plus 2 tablespoons dry white wine
   ¼ cup olive oil
   3 cups fresh spinach leaves, shredded
   2 cups coarsely chopped mushrooms
   1 cup grated carrots
   ⅓ cup sliced green onions
   2 cloves garlic, minced
   1 teaspoon *each* salt and onion powder
      Ground red pepper
      Ground white pepper
      Ground black pepper
3½ teaspoons garlic powder, divided
   1 cup dry bread crumbs
   1 teaspoon *each* dried basil, thyme and
      oregano
1½ cups Italian salad dressing
   ½ cup grated Parmesan cheese

Place chicken breasts in large shallow dish; add 2 cups wine. Cover; marinate in refrigerator at least 3 hours.

Heat oil in large skillet over medium heat. Add vegetables, salt, onion powder, ⅛ teaspoon *each* red and white pepper, ½ teaspoon black pepper, remaining 2 tablespoons wine and 1 teaspoon of the garlic powder. Cook and stir 3 to 5 minutes or until spinach is completely wilted; cool. Combine bread crumbs, remaining 2½ teaspoons garlic powder, the herbs, and ⅛ teaspoon *each* red, white and black pepper in shallow dish; set aside.

Preheat oven to 375°F. Slice a pocket in side of each chicken breast; fill with spinach mixture. Dip each filled breast into dressing, then place in bread crumb mixture. Spoon crumbs over chicken to cover completely. Place chicken in a single layer in greased baking pan. Drizzle with remaining dressing. Cover; bake 15 minutes. Uncover; bake 10 to 15 minutes or until slightly browned. Serve with cheese.

INDEX